# The Young Activist's
# DICTIONARY of
# SOCIAL
# JUSTICE

In collaboration with **RYSE TOTTINGHAM**
LGBTQ+ advocate and antibias, anti-racist educator

Illustrated by **ANDY PASSCHIER**

duopress

# LET'S LEARN THE VOCABULARY OF HUMAN RIGHTS

Dear reader,

Welcome to *The Young Activist's Dictionary of Social Justice*.

This isn't your usual dictionary—it is a tool made especially for you. Yes, it will define terms, like the difference between equity and equality, but this book is also full of stories about young activists just like you who saw something that needed to change and spoke up.

If you don't already know, you might be asking: What's an activist? For the official definition, you can look on page 3.

But right now, we'll let you in on a secret: YOU are an activist. Just because you picked up this book.

If you're looking at this page, you have the power to imagine a better world and create change. You are capable of using your voice and your influence for good.

We live in a world that is confusing and unfair sometimes. Some of the big issues that need fixing can seem much too big for one kid or even one adult. But as you'll see in this book, one person CAN make a big difference.

And why shouldn't that person be you?

## One note before you begin...

When we wrote this book, we chose words that are in use right now, but vocabulary can change over time. When in doubt, double-check!

If you have more questions about any of the words or subjects covered in this book, always do your research: Use multiple reliable sources to investigate and form your own opinion. Learning more about a topic will only make you stronger. And if something doesn't seem right or fair, keep asking questions. The only limit to learning is your curiosity!

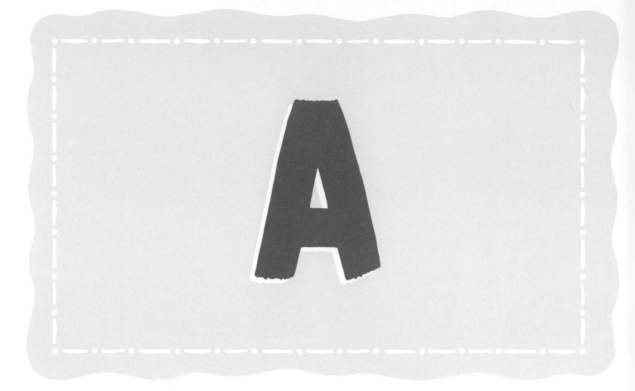

## ABILITY

uh BIL uh tee • noun

the skill, power, or quality of being capable of doing something

## ABLEISM

A buh li sem • noun

unfair or unjust treatment of people with disabilities (either on purpose or by accident)

## ABOLISH

uh BAH lish • verb

to do away with something or to get rid of it forever

## ABOLITION

aa buh LI shun • noun

the process of doing away with a practice or an institution; in U.S. history, it can refer to the movement that worked toward ending slavery

## ABOLITIONIST

aa buh LI shun ist • noun

someone who wants to get rid of slavery

## ACCENT

ACK sent • noun

stress on a particular part of a word, or the way in which someone speaks that's special to them or their region or culture

## ACCESS

ACK sess • noun

the right or freedom to be able to use something

## ACCESSIBILITY

ack sess eh BILL eh tee • adjective

the practice of making a tool or resource equally available to everyone

## ACCOMPLICE

aa COM pliss • noun

someone who gets involved to make change; also considered a step beyond ally (see below)

## ACCOUNTABILITY

uh COUNT eh bill eh tee • noun

holding yourself or someone else responsible (see page 46), or to account, for an action or for something said; knowing that your actions have consequences (see page 14) and owning up to them

## ACTIVE LISTENING

ACk tiv – LISS en ing • noun

a way of paying close attention to someone else when they are talking—includes looking them in the eyes, asking questions when you don't understand something they said, or responding to let the other person know you're interested in what they're talking about

## ACTIVISM

ACK tih vi sem • noun

the practice of taking action for or against a cause or an issue, with the hope of making a change to laws or to the way the public sees the cause or issue

## ACTIVIST

ACK tih vist • noun

someone who sees that something is wrong and stands up to do something about, or to draw attention to, whatever that is (you could also be an activist in favor of or in support of an issue)

## ADULTIFICATION

uh dull tiff ih CAY shun • noun

when kids are treated as though they are adults—this might mean that kids have to take on adult responsibilities when they're too young, or kids are being talked to and involved in conversations or decisions that should only be for adults

## ADVOCATE

AD voh kut • noun

someone who fights for or speaks up for another person and their cause (can also be used as a verb, to advocate for someone)

## AFFIRMATION

aa fur MAY shun • noun

a positive statement that builds confidence for yourself or for someone else, or the act of making this kind of statement

## AFFIRMING

uh FURM ing • verb

Saying positively that you believe something is true

*When it's attached to another word, it can mean that you recognize and support all forms of that word—for example, "gender-affirming" means that you recognize and want to support a person in their gender identity*

## AGEISM

AYJ ism • noun

unjust or unfair treatment against someone due to whatever age they are—old, young, or in between

## ALLY

AA lie • verb

someone who is united with and in support of another person's cause

## AMENDS

uh MENDZ • noun

an action or a payment made to make up for something wrong that was done to a person, or a loss or an injury that they might have had

## AMPLIFY

AM plih fie • verb

to make louder, particularly to make a voice from a marginalized community (see page 35) louder so that more people can hear it

## ANATOMY

uh NAH toh mee • noun

the physical and structural parts of the body

## ANCESTORS

ANN cess ters • noun

the people who came before you, often someone you are related to, going back many generations

## ANDROGYNOUS

ann DROH jin us • adjective

having characteristics that aren't specifically male or female, or looking or seeming partly male and partly female

## ANIMAL RIGHTS

ANN uh mull – RITES • plural noun

the belief that all animals should be treated fairly and that their rights should be considered just like humans' are

## ANTIBIAS

ant eye BYE us • adjective

working against bias (see page 7), working toward a community that celebrates differences and recognizes all parts of the human experience

## ANTIBLACK

ant eye BLAK • adjective

discriminating against, or showing hatred or opposition to, Black people because of their race

---

### PREFIXES: ANTI-

A prefix is a group of letters attached to the beginning of a word that change the meaning of that word. "Anti-" is a common prefix that means "against," and it comes up a lot in activist work. When it's at the front of the word, like "anti-racist," it means "against" that word, so in that case it's "against racism."

Some common words that start with "anti-" are:

ANTIBIAS (to act against bias)

ANTIBLACK (discrimination against Black people)

ANTI-RACIST (to act against racism)

ANTI-SEMITISM (discrimination against Jewish people)

The opposite of a prefix is a suffix, which is a group of letters attached to the end of a word.

# ANTI-RACIST

ant eye RAY sist • adjective

describes the process of actively looking for racism and working against it

# ANTI-SEMITISM

ant eye SEHM uh tih sem • noun

discriminating against, or showing hatred or opposition to, Jewish people because of their race or religion

# APARTHEID

uh PAR tied • noun

a government system that separated white people from people who weren't white, specifically referring to South Africa in the last half of the 20th century

# APPRECIATION

uh pre she A shun • noun

recognizing something or someone's value, or expressing gratitude for that person or thing

# APPROPRIATION

uh pro pree A shun • noun

to take something (for example, land or property, a style of dancing, a type of food, a symbol) and pretend it's your own or that it belongs to you, when you don't have a connection to it

# ARREST

uh REST • verb

to take to jail or prison (see The Littlest Marcher, page 6)

# APPRECIATION VS. APPROPRIATION

Learning about the history behind something from another culture and respecting other people and their cultures is extremely important.

Here are some questions to ask yourself to find out if you're appreciating or appropriating a certain thing:

- Do I know the history behind it?

- Have I ever talked to, or read something by, someone who is part of the original culture and learned why it is important to them?

- What is the result of me participating in, using, wearing, displaying, or having this thing? Does it benefit me or does it benefit the original culture?

- Am I being respectful of the people who first made or invented this? Am I giving proper credit?

- What is my motive: Am I interested in learning about another culture and connecting with the human beings who call that culture their own? Or am I just interested in borrowing for my own personal gain?

## ASEXUAL
### a SEK shoe ul • adjective

describes someone who expresses love romantically but not physically, or not in certain physical ways (which can be different for different individuals)

## ASSEMBLY
### uh SEM blee • noun

a group of people who come together in one place for the same reason

## ASSUMPTION
### uh SUMP shun • noun

believing something without asking any questions about it or finding out if you are right; a belief or idea that is not necessarily based on facts

## ASYLUM
### uh SYE luhm • noun

a place where someone can be protected and can take shelter; historically, a place where people who are mentally ill or differently abled, or others who need extra help, are confined and housed with assistance (not used as a positive term)

## AUTHENTIC
### awe THIN tick • adjective

something that is true, or something that is exactly what it says it is; also can mean being true to yourself

## AWARENESS
### uh WARE ness • noun

the ability to see or take note of your emotions, feelings, thoughts, and actions, or those of other people, especially to be able to see how those things affect others or a situation (also, see *self-awareness*, page 49)

## The Littlest Marcher

In 1963, **Audrey Faye Hendricks** was just nine years old when she made history as one of the youngest kids arrested during the Children's Crusade, or Children's March, to protest segregation in Birmingham, Alabama.

She and thousands of other children marched out of class and took to the streets to stand up for civil rights. These kids, trained in peaceful protest by Martin Luther King Jr., demonstrated because their parents couldn't—the adults' jobs, livelihoods, and lives were at stake if they protested. But what would happen to children who marched?

Audrey was arrested and held in jail for seven days, and so were hundreds of other kids. Meanwhile, the story of the brave young marchers was getting out. The rest of the country learned that the police had used dogs and firehoses to attack kids and had kept them in Juvenile Hall at the city jail. The outrage spurred pressure on leadership and helped end segregation laws in Birmingham.

Audrey later would be part of the first class of integrated students (see page 31) at the local high school.

## BALLOT

**BA lut • noun**

a piece of paper (or digital equivalent) where you mark down whom you are voting for in an election, usually in secret

## BAN

**BAAN • verb**

to stop someone from doing something or to make a rule that someone should not be doing an activity or using a particular item (like reading a specific book)

## BARRIER

**BEAR ee ur • noun**

a physical or symbolic wall or obstacle that is meant to keep something in or out, or to restrict anything going from one side of it to the other

## BI

**BYE • prefix**

as a prefix, *bi-* means "two" (see *bicultural, binary, biracial*), but when used to express orientation (see page 39) it can be short for *bisexual* (see next page)

## BIAS

**BYE us • noun**

when your personal opinion on something isn't based on reason, logic, or a previous experience

*When used as a verb, biases means to look at something with a biased view.*

## BICULTURAL

**bye CULL ture al • adjective**

from two different cultures

## BIGOT

**BIH gut • noun**

a person who hates anyone with a different opinion or culture from theirs

## BINARY

**BYE nare ee • noun**

divided into (or made up of) two separate or distinct parts

## BIPOC

**BYE pock • noun**

an acronym (a word that is made up of the first letters of other words) that stands for Black, Indigenous, (and) People of Color

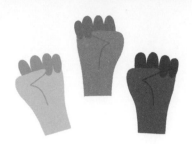

## BIRACIAL

**bye RAY shul • adjective**

having parents who are different races, or having to do with more than one race

## BISEXUAL

**bye SEK shoo all • adjective**

being sexually or romantically attracted to people who are the same sex as you, as well as people who are the opposite sex

# Standing Up for the Right to Sit

Before Rosa Parks famously refused to give up her seat on the bus to a white person, there was a younger activist who did the same thing, to much less fanfare: 15-year-old **Claudette Colvin**. One day she was riding on the segregated bus that took her to school. It had seats for white students at the front and black students at the back. When the bus got crowded, the black students were supposed to get up so that the white students could have a seat. Claudette was sitting down at the front of the black students' section when the bus driver asked her to give a white person her seat. She refused and was thrown off the bus by police, then arrested.

Her act of resistance was one of the first of its kind, nine months before Rosa Parks (more) famously did the same thing, also on a bus in Montgomery, Alabama. The actions of Colvin and Parks led to the Montgomery Bus Boycott, in which Black bus riders—about 40,000 people—stopped using the bus system. Since they made up most of the city's bus-riding population, this got people's attention. Colvin also joined a lawsuit that successfully got rid of bus segregation laws in Alabama.

Claudette Colvin later said, "History had me glued to my seat. It felt as though Harriet Tubman's hand was holding me down on one shoulder and Sojourner Truth was pushing me down on the other."

## BLACKFACE

**BLAK fayse • noun**

when a white person paints their face (or other body parts, like their hands) to make it look like they have black skin, especially historically, to mock or make fun of Black people

## BODY POSITIVITY

**BAH dee – pos ih TIV ih tee • noun**

the idea that all bodies are valid, accepted, and worthy of love and respect, no matter what they look like

## BOUNDARIES

**BOWN dah reez • noun**

visible or invisible borders or lines that should not be crossed; often used to mean personal boundaries: respecting rules another person sets about their own needs, or setting a limit or rule about your own physical or emotional needs

## BOYCOTT

**BOY cot • noun**

a nonviolent form of protest where one person or multiple people stop buying a certain product or using the services of a certain business, or avoid doing something in order to make a statement (see Standing Up for the Right to Sit, opposite)

## BRAVERY

**BRAY vuh ree • noun**

having courage or showing strength in the face of something scary or hard

## BULLYING

**BUH lee ing • verb**

purposefully hurting, picking on, or being mean to someone, either physically, mentally, socially, or online, sometimes over and over again as a pattern of behavior

## BYSTANDER

**BYE stan dur • noun**

a person who is present at an event or watching something happen, either in person or online, but who isn't part of it

## CAPITALISM
**CAP** ih tah li sem • noun

a system for dealing with money, in which people can buy and sell things and can form businesses that compete with other businesses to buy and sell products or services

## CENTERING
**SEN** ter ing • verb

intentionally making something the focus or subject of a conversation or presentation

## CHILD LABOR
**CHIULD – LAY** burr • noun

when a young person is forced into doing work or having a job, especially when there are specific laws against it; a form of modern-day slavery (see A Legacy of Bravery, opposite)

*Similar term: Bonded child labor occurs when children are forced to work to pay off a debt of money that was given to their parents.*

## CISGENDER
**SISS** jenn der • adjective

describes someone whose gender identity (see page 25) is the same as the sex that they were assigned at birth—for example, a person who identifies as male and has male sex organs, or a person who identifies as female and has female sex organs; sometimes shortened to *cis*

## CITIZENSHIP
**SIT** ih zen ship • noun

when someone lives in a town, state, or country and has membership and rights because of it

## CIVIL RIGHTS

**SIH vul – RYTES • noun**

basic rights (see page 47) that are given to a human being by the government of the country they live in; what the rights are can be spelled out in the governing documents of the country

*For example, in the United States, each individual has rights that are protected by the governing documents of the country: free speech, privacy, religion, assembly, a fair trial, and freedom of thought. What is considered a civil right can be defined differently depending on where you live.*

## CLASS

**KLAAS • noun**

a group of people who have about the same amount of money or same level of social status, as defined by their jobs, culture, religion, or the way their society is set up

## CLASSISM

**KLAA si sem • noun**

discrimination against someone because of their social status or wealth

## A Legacy of Bravery

**Iqbal Masih** was four years old when he began working at a loom in a carpet factory in Pakistan. He was sold into bonded child labor (see previous page) because his family needed to repay the carpet factory owner, who had loaned them money. Every day, Iqbal was literally chained to the loom, working all hours under abusive conditions.

Things changed when he ran away from work at the age of 10 and attended a meeting of the Bonded Labor Liberation Front, an organization that had already worked to make bonded labor illegal in Pakistan. Iqbal was surprised to learn that the government had cancelled debts that kept children working.

When he realized he was free, Iqbal got a letter from the government to send to the carpet factory where he had worked and then began attending school at the BLLF's Freedom Campus. He began educating other children about the laws against child labor and traveled to meet with rights activists from around the world, visiting Sweden and the United States to spread the word that slavery is still happening in the world.

But Iqbal's story has a tragic ending. In 1995, he was murdered in Pakistan. He was only 12 years old. After his death, he received the first World Children's Prize for the Rights of the Child, and he has become a symbol of the movement against child labor, which still goes on today.

## School Strike for Climate

**Greta Thunberg** began her protest of climate change at age 15. It all started with a simple act: standing by herself in front of the Swedish Parliament during school hours with a sign that read "School Strike for Climate." (Yes, she skipped school! With support from her parents and teachers, of course.)

She has now gone on to become a household name, address the United Nations, win the International Children's Peace Prize, sail across the Atlantic as part of a carbon-neutral transatlantic crossing, meet with the pope, and inspire 4 million people to join the largest climate strike in history in 2019.

The calm, clear, and unrelenting tone of her speeches and public statements (including her social media presence) has inspired a focus on climate change—so much that it has been called "the Greta Effect."

## CLIMATE CHANGE
### KLI met – CHAYNJ • noun

a long-lasting rise in air and water temperature in Earth's atmosphere and oceans (also known as global warming) due to human pollution (see School Strike for Climate, left)

## CLIMATE JUSTICE
### KLI met – JUSS tiss • noun

a movement that recognizes that climate change (see above) affects communities of color, underprivileged communities, and areas of lower socio-economic status the most and can make situations worse for them

*Climate justice is also known as environmental justice.*

## CLOSETED
### KLAH zeh ted • adjective

when a person's sexuality or gender identity is not public knowledge or has not been shared with others

## COALITION
### koh ah LIH shun • noun

an alliance of different people or groups coming together for action on one cause

## COLONIALISM
### kuh LOAH nee ah li sem • noun

when a single power (like a country or nation) asserts control over an area or a group of people who live outside its boundaries—usually a larger, more wealthy country over a smaller or less powerful one

*For example, the British monarchy, at the height of its power, ruled 23 percent of the world's population.*

## COLONIZATION

*koll oh ni ZAY shun • noun*

the process by which Europeans took control of lands across the world that were not originally theirs; colonization requires the mindset that the native peoples of a land are less human or less civilized than the colonizers and thus less worthy of land ownership

## COLONIZE

*KOLL oh nize • verb*

to take for your own or for your country; often refers to a group of people who claim a land that is not theirs and act like their rules and customs are the law of the land

## COLOR BLINDNESS

*KUH lor – BLYND ness • noun*

a way of looking at the world without acknowledging race or the way race impacts a particular situation or system

## COLORISM

*KUH luh ri sem • noun*

the favoring of lighter-skinned people over darker-skinned people, especially within the same ethnic or racial group

## COME OUT

*KUHM – OWT • verb*

to make your sexual orientation (see page 39) or gender identity (see page 25) public knowledge

## COMMUNITY

*kuhm YOU nih tee • noun*

a group of people with something in common, often living close to each other or sharing an interest

## COMPASSION

*kuhm PAA shun • noun*

being aware of someone else's struggle and having kindness for them, along with the desire to help

## CONFIRMATION BIAS

*kahn fer MAY shun – BYE us • noun*

the tendency to look for and prefer information that supports our existing beliefs or attitudes

## CONFORM

*kun FORM • verb*

to adhere to, to be similar to, or to act according to a societal custom

## CONSCIOUS

*KAHN shuss • adjective*

awake and aware, able to perceive or notice

## CONSCIOUS BIAS

*KAHN shuss – BYE us • noun*

attitudes that we are aware of that might influence the way we treat, think about, or interact with a particular group

## CONSENT

*kohn SENT • noun*

the giving of agreement to or approval of what someone else suggests that involves you; it requires a clear "yes" or "no"

## CONSEQUENCE

KAHN seh kwentz • noun

a result of a cause or an action

## CONSTRUCT

KOHN struct • noun

something created in people's minds that exists only in abstract terms or ideas

## CONTEXT

KOHN text • noun

the words used around a particular word, or situation around a particular occurrence, that might make the meaning clearer

## CONVENTIONAL

kun VEN shun ul • adjective

in agreement with what is normal, commonplace, or generally believed

## CONVERSATION

kohn vur SAY shun • noun

a dialogue, chat, talk, or verbal exchange of ideas

## CO-OPT

KOH–ahpt • verb

to take over or to force to be part of your group

*Co-opt is a synonym of appropriate (a form of appropriation, see page 5).

## COUNSELING

KOUN seh ling • noun

the giving of advice or guidance to someone to help them get through or manage a tough situation

## COURAGE

KER ij • noun

strength or bravery in the face of something scary

## CRIMINALIZATION

krim in ul eye ZAY shun • noun

when certain activities or behaviors are made illegal in order to turn one or more individuals into criminals

## CRIMINAL JUSTICE SYSTEM

KRIM in ul – JUSS tiss – SISS tehm • noun

a part of government whose job it is to enforce laws, determine whether someone has committed a crime, and punish people who have been found guilty

## CRIMINAL RECORD

KRIM in ul – REH kord • noun

a public statement/document that has information on past arrests (see page 5) or crimes; what goes on this record can depend on where you live

*When you apply for a job, the person or company that's hiring may check to see if you have one of these records. If you have been unfairly arrested or convicted, it can affect your chances of getting the job.

## CRISIS

CRY sis • noun

an unstable moment when an impactful or important change may be about to happen, especially when there is a chance of disaster or a bad ending if things don't go the right way

## CRITICAL RACE THEORY
**KRI tick ul – RAYSE – THEER ee • noun**

a way of looking at history, through the lens of race and racism (see page 44), that connects the dots between oppressive, socially created laws and systems in the past and what is happening in the present

*Critical race theory is a type of critical thinking taught in college or law school classes. It's not the same as antibias or anti-racist education!*

## CRITICAL THINKING
**KRI tick ul – THINK ing • noun**

the using of your senses, your brain, and what you already know to ask questions, get curious (see below), and dig deeply into information about a subject, topic, or something in the world around you

## CULTURAL INTELLIGENCE
**KULL cher ul – ihn TELL ih gentz • noun**

the ability to hold space for and interact with people from other cultures who might have different beliefs or traditions

## CULTURE
**KULL cher • noun**

a set of beliefs, attitudes, traditions, perspectives, values (see page 55), and/ or practices that are unique to one group of people, including but not limited to language, objects, rituals, and art, passed down from one generation to the next

## CURIOUS
**KYUR ee us • adjective**

when you take an interest in or want to learn more about a particular thing

## DEBUNK

**dee BUNK • verb**

to reveal a falsehood about a statement, idea, or event that was presented as true or fact

## DECENCY

**DEE sen see • noun**

the quality of being kind to or having goodwill or good manners toward other people or treating someone with respect

## DECOLONIZE

**dee COLL oh nize • verb**

to free someone, something, or a group of people from control by another country or group

## DEFUND

**dee FUND • verb**

to take money from something and give it away elsewhere, or to prevent something from getting more money

*Defunding is often part of the conversation in cities that have money specifically set aside for police. The movement to defund the police can mean different things (from reducing their workload to abolishing the police entirely), but the goal of the cause is to take money that is being used to fund police activity and re-invest it into community programs. Services that are allocated to police might be better handled by other professionals—for example, a mental health professional could respond to someone having a mental health crisis, or a professional social worker might check in on the homeless.*

## DEMOCRACY

di MAH kreh see • noun

a form of government where the people are represented at the highest level and the majority decides the rules

## DEMONSTRATION

deh muhn STRAY shun • noun

a gathering of a group of people to act, march, or rally for or against a cause

## DESTRUCT

dee STRUCKT • verb

to take apart; to damage beyond repair

## DIALOGUE

DYE ah log • noun

a conversation, debate, or discussion between two or more people

## DIASPORA

dye AH spoh ra • noun

a community of people living or settled down outside their original home or homeland; also refers to the place where this community lives

*For example: The community of Jewish people or Israelites living outside Israel can be called a diaspora. The African diaspora includes anyone who can claim descent from the continent of Africa but lives elsewhere.*

## DICTATOR

DIK tay tor • noun

someone who governs or rules with complete authority

## DIE-IN

DYE – IN • noun

a demonstration or protest in which people lie on the ground as if they are dead

*Also can be called a lie-in.*

## DIGNITY

DIG nuh tee • noun

the state of having worth and of deserving honor and respect

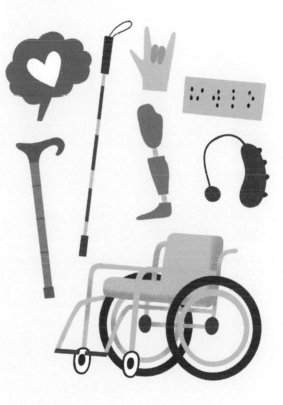

## DISABILITY

diss uh BILL ih tee • noun

a state of being that makes it difficult to see, hear, walk, talk, read, learn, or do other things that are important to life

*There is a wide range of different types of disabilities—they can be physical or mental or both, they can be forever or temporary, and they also can be from birth or caused by an injury.*

# DISCOMFORT

diss COME fert • noun

a feeling of being uneasy or distressed about something

# DISCRIMINATE

diss CRIM in ate • verb

to treat one or more people unfairly, usually because of a foundational part of their identity, such as sex, religion, race, culture, or country of origin

# DISENFRANCHISE

diss in FRAN chyze • verb

to take away or withhold rights, specifically the right to vote; also, being powerless or voiceless in your community (as in, disenfranchised youth)

# DISMANTLE

diss MAN tull • verb

to take apart; to completely break up or separate

# DISPARITY

diss PARE ih tee • noun

a condition or situation of being noticeably unequal or of being distinctly different from a societal norm

# DISRUPT

diss RUPT • verb

to challenge, break apart, or cause major change or disorder

# DIVERSITY

die VER sih tee • noun

when people with different backgrounds, races, ethnicities, religions, abilities, and other identities are well represented within a group

# Life Without School?

As a young girl, it wasn't always safe for **Malala Yousafzai** to go to school. The Taliban had taken control of the village where she lived in northern Pakistan. Under their law, schools for girls were ordered to close or were burned down. But Malala was determined to continue her education. She spoke out publicly, publishing a record of her diary on the BBC Urdu.

It didn't take long for her activism to draw the attention and ire of the Taliban. In October of 2012, a gunman climbed aboard her school bus. He attempted to assassinate Malala, shooting her in the head at point-blank range. Yet somehow, she survived, escaped to England, and made a miraculous recovery.

The frightening attempt on her life seemed to boost Malala's courage. She established a charity called the Malala Fund, dedicated to education for girls. At age 17, she became the youngest winner of the Nobel Peace Prize and went on to graduate from Oxford. She continues to fight for education—and the 130 million girls across the globe who should have equal access to it.

## ECOLOGY
ee KAH luh gee • noun

the environment, or the relationship between organisms and their environment

## ECONOMY
ee KOHN eh me • noun

the way goods and services are created, distributed, sold, and used in a particular region

## EDUCATION
eh djeh CAY shun • noun

the process of learning, going to school, getting formal instruction, or being taught (see Life Without School?, opposite)

## EGALITARIANISM
ee gah lih TARE ee ah ni sem • noun

the belief that all humans are equal

## EGO
EE goh • noun

how you feel about yourself, especially when comparing yourself to other people

## ELECTED OFFICIALS
eh LECK ted – oh FISH uhls • noun

individuals who are chosen by the people to represent them in government

## ELECTION
eh LECK shun • noun

the process of choosing someone through voting

## EMANCIPATE
eh MAN sih payte • verb

to set free from enslavement, bondage, or the power or control of another person or governing body

## Little Miss Flint

In April 2015, the city of Flint, Michigan, switched its water supply from the Detroit water system to the nearby Flint River in an effort to save money.

Within a few months, people in the area started feeling sick—they had rashes, some people were losing their hair, and others just noticed that the water looked, smelled, and tasted funny. However, community leaders insisted that the water was safe.

After more than a year of complaints, a group of doctors investigated and ran blood tests on the children of Flint. They found that lead levels in the blood were off-the-charts high. (Lead is dangerous because it can cause serious developmental problems.) But the government still refused to take action.

It was then that eight-year-old **Mari Copeny**, aka Little Miss Flint, took matters into her own hands. She wrote a letter to President Barack Obama asking him to visit Flint and see the water crisis first-hand. After this visit, he approved $100 million in relief for the city.

Mari continues to use her platform to fight for clean water in Flint and to fundraise and champion causes like environmental racism.

## EMANCIPATION
eh man sih PAY shun • noun

the act of freeing from bondage or enslavement, particularly referring to the Emancipation Proclamation of 1863, which declared that all enslaved peoples in the United States should be set free

## EMOTIONAL INTELLIGENCE
uh MOH shun al – in TELL ih gents • noun

the ability to know what emotions you're feeling, as well as understanding what emotions others might be having

## EMPATHY
EM puh thee • noun

the ability to look at someone else's situation or experience and imagine or share the feelings that they might be having

## EMPOWER
im POW ur • verb

to inspire or give power to someone so they can grow into their own abilities or talents and believe in themselves

## ENGAGEMENT
en GAYGE ment • noun

the act of paying attention to or actively participating in something; also the number of people doing so

## ENSLAVED PEOPLE

en SLAYVD – PEE pull • noun

human beings who are "owned" by other human beings, are not allowed to have free will, and receive no compensation for the work they do

*Using the phrase enslaved people instead of slaves emphasizes that these human beings were people first, not property, and that they were in bondage against their will and because of other human beings.*

## ENVIRONMENTAL JUSTICE

in vye er MEN tull – JUSS tiss • noun

the idea that no group of people should be unfairly affected by the negative environmental impact of entities like businesses, industries, or governments (see Little Miss Flint, opposite)

## EQUALITY

ee KWA lih tee • noun

the quality of being the same in some measurable way or just as good as

## EQUITY

EH kwi tee • noun

justice for and fair treatment of people regardless of who they are or what group they belong to

## ERASE

uh RASE • verb

to make invisible; to remove from a narrative or from history

## ESCALATE

EH sku late • verb

to make more intense

## ETHNICITY

eth NISS ih tee • noun

belonging to a group of people with the same racial, national, religious, or cultural customs

## EXCLUSION

ik SKLU shun • noun

the act of leaving out or preventing from being a part of

## EXTREMIST

ik STREEM ist • adjective

having views that are very different from what most people consider to be reasonable, including opposition to certain basic values such as democracy, liberty, and respect of others

### EQUALITY VS. EQUITY

Equality sounds pretty good, right? It's when everyone is the same and is treated exactly alike.

However, there is a difference between the ideas of equality and equity. Unlike equality, equity takes the effects of privilege and prejudice into account.

Equity means that people are given what they need according to their circumstances. Equality means that everyone is given the same thing regardless of circumstances. (It's similar to the comparison of fair vs. equal on page 23.) In a world that's still working toward equality, the way to justice is through equity.

## FAIR
FEHR • *adjective*

when all are treated equally and honestly; free from bias, prejudice, or favoritism

## FASCISM
FAA shi zum • *noun*

a political view that says that the nation is more important than the individual

## FAT ACTIVISM
FAT – ACK tih vi sem • *noun*

a social movement that opposes discrimination against overweight people

*Also called* fat acceptance.

## FEEDBACK
FEED bak • *noun*

helpful information or input about how to change something for the better

## FEMINISM
FEH meh ni sem • *noun*

the belief that men and women are equal

*Many generations of women have fought—and continue to fight—for women's rights, including the right to vote, the right to go to work or school, the right to make the same amount of money as men do, the right to live free from violence and discrimination, and much more.*

## FEMINIST
FEH meh nist • *noun*

someone who believes that men and women are equal and advocates for equality when they see inequality

## FLUID

FLOO ihd • adjective

not fixed, not permanent, able to be changed

*For example, a person who is gender fluid is someone whose gender identity or expression may change over time.*

## FOLKS

FOKES • noun

a gender-neutral way to refer to more than one person or a group of people

*The alternative spelling folx may be used to make it clear that you are including marginalized people in the group you're talking about.*

### FAIR VS. EQUAL

Sometimes fair is not the same as equal, and that's okay.

If you are tall, you may not need a stepping stool to reach a snack on the counter—you might be able to reach it without help. But your friend might not be able to reach it at their height.

Fairness is giving a step stool to your shorter friend so that both of you can reach, and have access to, the same snack on the counter.

When everyone gets what they need, that's fairness. When everyone gets the exact same thing, that's equality. What is equal is not always fair. What kind of world would you want to live in—one that's fair or one that's equal?

## FOOD DESERT

FUUD – DEH zurt • noun

a place where it is hard to find fresh produce to buy within the area

## FOOD INSECURITY

FUUD – in sih KYUR ih tee • noun

inconsistent access or ability to get enough food because of a lack of money or another resource

## FOOD PANTRY

FUUD – PAN tree • noun

a place where food is donated and can be given away to people who need it

## FUNDAMENTALISM

fun dah MEN ta li sem • noun

a movement or set of beliefs that gives importance to the strict loyalty to and literal interpretation of a text or set of principles

## GASLIGHT
### GAAS lyte • verb

to try to manipulate someone by telling them that something they know is true is not true, or something that they are feeling is not real

## GATEKEEPER
### GAYT kee pur • noun

someone who has the power to control access; it can be exclusion from a physical space or a particular individual, or from participation in a conversation, therefore leaving out individuals or smaller communities that should belong

## GAY
### GAE • adjective

describes men who are sexually or romantically attracted to other men; also used as a catchall term for anyone who is attracted to members of the same sex

## GENDER
### JENN der • noun

characteristics that are associated with a particular sex, such as male or female; however, someone's gender could be male, female, or a range of identities that do not relate to male or female

*The system of sorting people into either the male or the female gender is called the gender binary.*

## GENDER EXPRESSION
### JENN der – ex PREH shun • noun

the ways someone shows their gender identity through physical characteristics or behaviors

## GENDER IDENTITY

JENN der – eye DEN tih tee • noun

the gender that a person identifies with based on what they know about themselves (through their internal, individual life)

*A person's gender or gender identity does not have to match and does not relate to their sex, and it also is not impacted by their gender expression (such as the clothes they choose to wear or the pronouns they choose).

## GENDER ROLE

JENN der – ROHL • noun

an idea of what kinds of tasks, jobs, or other activities a person of a particular gender should be involved with

*A behavioral example of a gender role is the idea that boys should play with trucks and girls should play with dolls.

## GENERATIONAL

jeh ne RAY shun al • adjective

having to do with something passed down by parents, older relatives, or ancestors

## GENERATIONAL TRAUMA

jeh ne RAY shun al – TRAAH ma • noun

pain or hurt that is experienced by multiple generations or passed down from parents to children

## GENOCIDE

JEN oh side • noun

intentional murder of people from a particular racial, ethnic, religious, political, or cultural group

## GENTRIFICATION

jen trih fih CAY shun • noun

when people who are middle class or wealthy move to a poorer neighborhood and eventually cause the poorer people to move out when it becomes too expensive to live there

## GLOBALISM

GLOW buh li sem • noun

the belief that people, goods, and information should be able to travel freely across borders

## GLOBAL MAJORITY

GLOW bul – muh JORE ih tee • noun

refers to the Black people, Indigenous people, and people of color who make up more than 80% of the world's population

## GRASSROOTS

GRAAS roots • adjective

describes the most basic level of society, or everyday people; often used to define a movement that has spread through engagement of individuals within the community

## Schools Should Be Safe

On February 14, 2018, 17 people at Marjory Stoneman Douglas High School in Parkland, Florida, were murdered when a gunman opened fire on students and staff.

Many students came out of this life-changing event demanding change from their representatives at all levels of government. One of them was **X González**, who made headlines for their speech at an anti-gun rally in Ft. Lauderdale, FL. X cofounded the advocacy group Never Again MSD. This organization worked with the nonprofit Everytown for Gun Safety to organize a demonstration called March for Our Lives in 2018, a little over a month after the Parkland shooting. It was one of the biggest youth protests since the era of the Vietnam War and raised millions of dollars to fight gun violence.

The hashtags #NeverAgain and #EnoughIsEnough became symbols of the movement.

## GRIT

GRIT • *noun*

perseverance; working toward a goal with determination and despite hardship

*This term describes a resilient quality in someone's character. Sometimes it can be problematic, if it's used to talk about poverty and the hardships that some kids have had to face—whether they wanted to or not.*

## GUN CONTROL

GUHN – kun TROL • *noun*

the attempt to make laws that regulate who is able to buy or own guns or firearms

*Different countries have different rules about who can own guns. The Canadian government allows people to have rifles or shotguns but strongly restricts handguns. Germany requires background checks for everyone who wants to buy a gun (and they have to be over 18).*

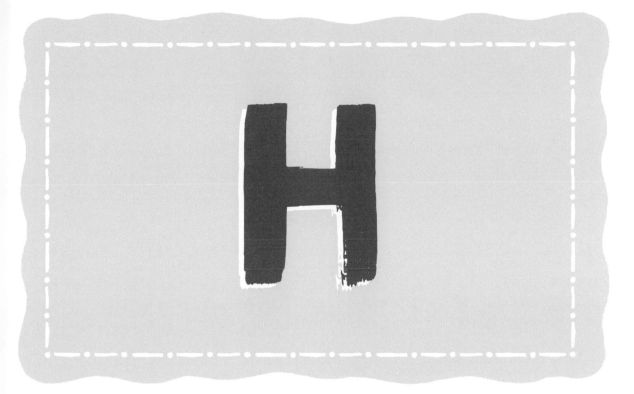

## HARASSMENT

huh RASS ment • noun

unwanted verbal or physical behavior that creates an unpleasant or dangerous situation for someone

## HARM REDUCTION

HARM – re DUC shun • noun

practices that try to reduce the damage of drug use by treating drug users with compassion

## HATE CRIME

HAYT – CRYM • noun

a crime that is motivated by hatred of a person's race, ethnicity, religion, orientation, gender, or other identifying characteristics

## HEGEMONY

HEDJ eh moh nee • noun

the influence of a dominant group of people

## HERITAGE

HEHR ih tedj • noun

property or traditions passed down to the next generation

## HETERONORMATIVE

heh teh roh NOR mah tiv • adjective

describes the idea that heterosexuality is the only normal or acceptable version of sexuality

## HETEROSEXUAL

heh teh roh SEK shoo al • adjective

describes someone who is attracted sexually or romantically to members of the opposite sex

## HIERARCHY

HIE er are kee • noun

a ranking system

## HIJAB

*hih JAAB • noun*

a traditional head wrap or head covering that is worn by Muslim women

## HIJRA

*HIDJ ruh • noun*

a third gender recognized in Hindu culture and one of the oldest third-gender communities in the world; usually refers to people who identify as women but were assigned male at birth

## HISTORY

*HIH stoh ree • noun*

an account or record of the past or of past events

*Usually written by the dominant culture or the group that emerged victorious.*

## HOMOPHOBIA

*hoh moh FO bee ah • noun*

fear of or discrimination against homosexual people

## HOMOSEXUAL

*hoh moh SECK shoo al • adjective*

describes someone who is attracted sexually or romantically to members of the same sex

## HUMANITARIAN

*hyu MAN ih tare ee an • noun*

someone who has decided it is their job to fight for social justice or the well-being of other humans

## HUMANITY

*hyu MAN ih tee • noun*

mankind or all human beings; also means being compassionate

## HUMANIZE

*HYU man ize • verb*

to see or portray someone in a way that reminds others that they are a human being and an individual

## HUMAN RIGHTS

*HYU man – RYTES • noun*

basic rights that belong to every human being just because they are a human being

*For example, the right to live safely as a free person and the right to have food and shelter.*

## HYGIENE

*HY geen • noun*

the act of keeping up with your cleanliness and wellness to remain healthy

## IDEA

**eye DEE uh • noun**

a thought, opinion, or something that is imagined or seen in the mind

## IDENTIFY

**eye DEN tih fye • verb**

to say what you are, or to recognize someone or something as being an individual person or particular place or thing

## IDENTITY

**eye DEN tih tee • noun**

who you are, or the characteristics that make one person recognizable or distinct as an individual person

## IGNORANCE

**IG noh runce • noun**

having no understanding or awareness of a subject

## ILLEGAL

**ih LEE gul • adjective**

not allowed because of a rule or law

## IMMIGRANT

**IHM ih grunt • noun**

someone who moves to another country to settle there permanently

*The act of becoming an immigrant or moving to another country to live is called immigration.*

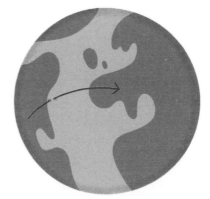

## IMPACT

**IHM packt • noun**

the effect something has on a person, thing, or event

## IMPERIALISM

**ihm PEER ee ah li sem • noun**

when one nation asserts its power over other parts of the world, either directly or indirectly

### IMPACT VS. INTENT

**"They had the best intentions!"** Have you ever heard someone say this phrase?

Think about a time when you might have had good intentions, but something went wrong. What was the impact of your actions? Did they have more of an effect than your intentions?

Although intent is important, it's often not what other people see. Impact is a direct result of actions, and it can make people have certain feelings. For example, maybe two friends are having a conversation, and one friend makes a joke about the other friend's hair. Even though the joke wasn't supposed to be mean (intent), the second friend feels sad (impact).

## IMPLICIT

**ihm PLI sit • adjective**

not consciously known about, or something that is understood even though it's not specifically said

*For example, implicit bias (like unconscious bias) is a prejudice that is present without thought or intent.*

## IMPOSTER SYNDROME

**ihm POSS ter – sin DROME • noun**

the belief that you don't know how to do something despite evidence that you do, or the fear of being shown to be an impostor (someone who assumes a fake identity or tries to trick) despite your success

## INCARCERATION

**ihn CAR sir ay shun • noun**

the act of putting someone in prison

## INCLUSION

**ihn KLU shun • noun**

the act of making something or someone part of a group or meaningfully involving someone in something

*Inclusive is an adjective that derives from inclusion. You may have heard of inclusive language, which is language that is thoughtful in the way it refers to other people. Some words or expressions may exclude certain groups of people, like the word mankind. An inclusive way of saying the same thing is to use the word humankind.*

## INCOME INEQUALITY

**IHN kum – ihn ee KWAL ih tee • noun**

when two people are paid different amounts for the same work; also how income is unevenly spread through a group of people

## Paving the Way

In 1954, the Supreme Court of the United States declared that southern states could not keep schools segregated—that is, it was no longer legal to separate Black and white children into different schools.

At William Frantz Elementary School in New Orleans, Louisiana, it meant a new student would be enrolling: **Ruby Bridges**. When she was just six, Ruby became one of the first Black students to attend an integrated elementary school in the southern United States.

On a fall day in November, she walked in with four U.S. marshals for her protection. Ruby was ostracized and taunted on her way to school, and only one teacher was willing to educate her, so she ended up in a classroom by herself with Mrs. Barbara Henry. She couldn't even go to the bathroom without an escort. Despite these obstacles, she graduated from high school and went on to become a travel agent and have a family.

Ruby's bravery as a young girl inspired a famous painting called *The Problem We All Live With*, by Norman Rockwell.

## INDIGENOUS

*ihn DIH gin us • adjective*

describes an original inhabitant of a certain land; native to a particular place

## INEQUALITY

*ihn ee KWAL ih tee • noun*

the state of being unequal or uneven; the opposite of equality (see page 21)

## INNATE

*ihn NAYT • adjective*

naturally occurring or already present in something

## INQUISITIVE

*ihn KWIZ ih tihv • adjective*

having curiosity (see page 15); prone to asking questions

## INSENSITIVE

*ihn SEHN sih tihv • adjective*

not considering the feelings of others

## INSPIRATION

*ihn spih RAY shun • noun*

something that moves someone to action, sparks their creativity, gives them an idea, or makes them feel excited

## INTEGRATION

*ihn teh GRAY shun • noun*

the weaving of two things together, but specifically when two parts of society become one group

*Integration is also used to describe a time when segregation of schools was no longer lawful and Black students began attending schools that were previously made up of only white students.*

## INTEGRITY
*ihn TEH grih tee • noun*

staying true to a code of morals or values

## INTENT
*ihn TENT • noun*

what you meant or planned to happen

## INTERGENERATIONAL
*ihn tur jen ur AYSH un al • adjective*

spanning or going across multiple generations

## INTERNATIONALISM
*ihn ter NASH un al ih sem • noun*

the idea that countries and nations around the world should cooperate with each other

## INTERPRET
*ihn TUR prit • verb*

to translate or explain the meaning of something

## INTERRACIAL
*ihn tur RAY shul • adjective*

involving two people who are of different races

*\*Interracial marriage is a marriage between two people who are different races.*

## INTERSECTIONALITY
*ihn tur sek shun AL ih tee • noun*

the idea that all oppression is connected and that when there is an overlap of certain identifying traits that are oppressed, like race, sex, religion, ethnicity, ability, sexual orientation, etc., there is a unique disadvantage

## INTERSEX
*IHN tur seks • noun*

a term that can represent a range of identities or situations in which a person is born with sexual anatomy that is not just male or female

## JUDGMENT

JUDJ ment • noun

an opinion that is formed after careful thought and examination

## JUDGMENTAL

judj MEN tull • adjective

characterized by forming an opinion too harshly and too quickly

## JUSTICE

JUSS tiss • noun

fair treatment; upholding what is deserved, right, good, and lawful

## JUSTIFY

JUSS tih fie • verb

to provide reasons for doing something

## KINDNESS

KYND nehs • noun

the treatment of people with respect and consideration

## KINSHIP

KIHN ship • noun

being in the same family, having a common ancestor, or having a close connection to someone

## LANGUAGE

LAAN gwij • noun

a system of expression through words

## LATINX

la tih NEKS • adjective

a gender-neutral alternative spelling of *Latino* or *Latina* (someone of Latin American heritage)

## LAWSUIT

LAW soot • noun

a case brought before a court of law

## LEADER

LEE der • noun

someone who shows the way or guides other people

## LEARNING DIFFERENCES

LER ning – DIFF ren sez • noun

a term to replace *learning disability* that focuses on the fact that some people simply learn differently than others, rather than having some inherent "disability" or "disorder"

## LEGACY

LEH gah see • noun

an inheritance, gift, or tradition passed down from an ancestor or someone who came before

## LESBIAN

LEZ bee in • noun

a woman who is attracted sexually or romantically to other women

## LIBERATION

lih beh RAY shun • noun

the act of setting something or someone free; can also refer to a movement that seeks equal rights

## LITERACY

LIH teh rah see • noun

the ability to read and write

## LOOPHOLE

LUUP hohl • noun

an uncertainty in or unclear part of a text through which the text's rules or intended laws can be avoided or worked around

# Reading for Freedom

It might seem like reading is a skill that everyone these days learns in school. But when **Frederick Bailey** was a young enslaved man, he was forbidden any kind of education, including reading and writing.

At an early age, Frederick taught himself to read and write. It was the beginning of a lifetime of activism. Teaching others to read, when he was just 16, was the moment he empowered others.

Eventually he fled captivity successfully, disguising himself as a sailor with the help of his future wife, Anna. He changed his last name to Douglass and became an abolitionist, orator, and intellectual. He was so accomplished that some of his contemporaries suggested that his speech might be too polished or too "white" to be believed.

Literacy, he said, was "a new and special revelation, explaining dark and mysterious things, with which my youthful understanding had struggled, but struggled in vain." It was the pathway to his freedom.

## MANSPLAIN

### MAN splayn • verb

when a man explains something to another person (female or nonbinary) in a superior way, assuming that they don't know anything about the topic

## MARGINALIZE

### MAR jih nuh lize • verb

to make a person or group powerless or unimportant

## MELANIN

### MELL uh nihn • noun

a pigment in a living creature that causes color (black, brown, reddish, or yellow) in the skin, hair, feathers, or eyes

*Someone with high melanin content in their skin can be described as melanated.*

## MICROAGGRESSION

### MYE crow uh gre shun • noun

a small or seemingly insignificant action that occurs consciously or unconsciously and demonstrates racist, misogynist, or other hateful behavior toward a person

## MIGRANT

### MYE grunt • noun

someone who moves to another country to live there temporarily

## MINDFULNESS

### MYND full nes • noun

the quality of being aware of your surroundings, emotions, or thoughts in the moment

## MINORITY

mye NORE ih tee • noun

someone who is not part of the dominant group

## MISOGYNOIR

mih sah jeh NWAR • noun

hatred of, or prejudice against, Black women

## MISOGYNY

mih SAH jeh nee • noun

hatred of, or prejudice against, women

## MIXED

mikst • adjective

short for *mixed race*; having ancestors that are two or more races

## MODEL MINORITY

MAH dul – mye NOR ih tee • noun

the stereotypical view that people of Asian and Pacific Islander descent are smart and excel at whatever they do, especially as compared to Black and Indigenous people

## MONOLITH

MAH no lith • noun

a group of individuals who are all considered the same

## MORALITY

moh RA lih tee • noun

guidelines for living that are based on beliefs about what behavior is right and what behavior is wrong

## MOVEMENT

MOOV mint • noun

organized activities or events working toward one goal

## MULTIETHNIC

mull tee ETH nick <u>or</u> mull tie ETH nick • adjective

belonging to or having ancestors who come from more than one ethnicity

## MULTIRACIAL

mull tee RAY shul <u>or</u> mull tie RAY shul • adjective

belonging to or having ancestors who come from more than one race

## MUTUAL AID

MYOO choo ul – AYD • noun

an exchange of resources and services between people who want to help each other

## MYTH

mith • noun

an imaginary story, person, or thing, sometimes created to explain a history, belief, or event

# N

## NATIVE
### NAY tihv • noun

someone who was born in the same land they are currently living in

## NATIVISM
### NAY tih vi sem • noun

promoting or favoring the interests of people already living in a place over people who immigrated to the area

## NEGOTIATE
### neh GO shee ate • verb

to have a discussion and arrive at an agreement or settle a matter

## NEURODIVERSITY
### nure oh dye VER sih tee • noun

the idea that people's brains learn to function in many different ways, and that variation in brain function is normal; the inclusion of all types of thinking and communicating

*Neurodiversity welcomes all types of brain function without stigma. For example, that means that people who have autism or ADHD shouldn't be treated as though they have a "disorder."*

## NEUTRAL
### NEW trull • adjective

describes a group, person, or entity that does not take a side in a debate or conflict

## An Icon from Age 15

**John Lewis** was a civil rights icon, leader, and U.S representative, but he didn't start out that way. When he was a kid, he used to practice giving sermons to the roost of chickens on his family's farm. (He loved them so much that he performed chicken weddings and funerals!)

All of this practice paid off when he wrote and delivered his first sermon to people at age 15, sparking a life of public service. Lewis was greatly impacted by the Civil Rights Movement in Alabama and the integration of Alabama's schools—he once said that the sermon was inspired by Autherine Lucy, a woman who was applying to be the first black student at the University of Alabama.

## NONBINARY

naan BYE na ree • adjective

having a gender identity that does not fall exclusively into either the category "man" or "woman"; includes a wide range of identities

## NONPROFIT

naan PRAH fit• adjective

a company or organization with a purpose that is something other than making money

## NONVIOLENCE

naan VIE eh lence • noun

the practice of choosing not to use violence as a tactic and matter of principle

*The principle of nonviolence was an essential part of the Civil Rights Movement of the 1960s in the United States (see An Icon from Age 15, left), but one of the most famous leaders practicing nonviolence was Mohandas K. Gandhi. Gandhi fought against the British oppression in his native India and is considered a pioneer of using nonviolence as resistance.*

## NORMALIZE

NOR mah lyze • verb

to make more standard or commonplace

## NUANCE

NOO ahnse • noun

a small difference or variation

## OBSERVATION
ahb ser VAY shun • noun

careful watching or studying to notice something or gather information

## OCCUPATION
ah kew PAY shun • noun

when one state or country has control over another country and has a military presence there

## OPEN-MINDED
OH pehn – MYNE did • adjective

able to receive new ideas or opinions

## OPPRESSION
oh PREH shun • noun

unjust or cruel treatment

## ORGANIZATION
or gah nih ZAY shun • noun

a business, association, society, charity, nonprofit, or other group created for a purpose

## ORGANIZER
or gah NYE zer • noun

someone who plans or coordinates an event (see The Young Organizer, page 40)

## ORIENTATION
or ee ehn TAY shun • noun

short for *sexual orientation*; someone's sexual identity or preference, that is, whom someone is attracted to

## The Young Organizer

When **Clara Lemlich** was a young girl, she fled Ukraine with her Eastern European Jewish family to settle in New York. Her hometown wasn't safe for Jews anymore—organized massacres called pogroms were destroying lives and homes.

After they arrived, Clara, who was 17, quickly found herself working in a garment shop, just two weeks after her arrival. The working hours were long— six days a week, 11 hours a day— wages were low at $3 per week, and conditions were harsh and dangerous.

She immediately took action, delivering rousing speeches, leading her union, marching in picket lines, and writing articles about the factory conditions. In 1909, she led a strike of shirtwaist makers who walked out of their jobs for two months to protest wages and conditions. This strike, later called The Uprising of the 20,000, was partially successful in achieving better pay and shorter hours, but it also showed how effective women and girls could be when they participated in strikes.

## OTHER

**UH** *ther* • *noun*

one on the outside, not included, or different

## OUT

*owt* • *adjective*

short for *out of the closet* (see page 12); someone whose sexual identity or orientation is known publicly

## WHAT'S AN ACRONYM?

You may have heard the letters LGBTQ+ being used to refer to certain people and their sexual orientation. Here's what those letters mean!

L = lesbian (see page 34)

G = gay (see page 24)

B = bisexual (see page 8)

T = trans (see page 53)

Q = queer or questioning (see page 44)

+ = other types of sexual identities not listed; represents and includes the great diversity of the community

Sometimes the acronym is expanded to include:

2S = two-spirit (see page 54)

I = intersex (see page 32)

A = asexual (see page 6)

# PANSEXUAL

**paan SEK shoo al • adjective**

describes someone who is sexually or romantically attracted to people regardless of their gender identity or sex

# PARTICIPANT

**pahr TISS ih pent • noun**

a person who takes part in an event, activity, or doing something with others

# PASSING

**PAA sing • noun**

the ability of someone to appear to belong to a different identity or racial or ethnic group, which may result in privilege or social acceptance

# PATRIARCHY

**PAY tree ar kee • noun**

a group that is governed by a male leader or father; more broadly, the way that society is structured to keep men (particularly white men) at the top and in power

# PATRIOTISM

**PAY tree uh ti sem • noun**

love of country

# PERCEPTION

pur SEP shun • noun

the way in which an individual sees the world

*Your perception of an event might be different than someone else's perception of it.

# PERFORMATIVE

pur FOR mah tiv • adjective

describes something done for show or for the purpose of making yourself look good

# PERPETUATE

pur PEH chu ate • verb

to continue or to keep something going

# PETITION

peh TISH un • noun

a document with signatures that support a call for change

# PHOBIA

FO bee ah • noun or suffix

extreme hatred or fear of an object or situation; when used as a suffix, a hatred or fear of a type of people (who are usually different than you)

*In other usage, phobia might describe a condition where someone is fearful about a particular object or situation (like spiders or heights), but in social justice terms it's often a suffix (see page 4) referring to a specific hatred of a group of people. For example: Islamophobia is phobia of Muslims; transphobia is phobia of trans people; homophobia is phobia of gay people; fat phobia is phobia of fat people, and so on.

# POC

abbreviation

acronym that stands for Person (or People) of Color (see also BIPOC, page 8)

# POLICING

puh LEE sing • verb

controlling or enforcing laws with the use of police or an official government force

# POLLUTION

puh LOO shun • noun

harm done to the environment by people

# POVERTY

PAH vur tee • noun

the condition of being poor and unable to get basic needs for yourself (like buying food or providing shelter)

# POWER

POW er • noun

control or authority over others; also, strength

# PREJUDICE

PREDJ eh dis • noun

unfair judgment against a person, group, culture, religion, etc.

# PRIDE

PRYD • noun

parades, rallies, or events held to celebrate the LGBTQ+ community and their fight for equality

*Pride Month is held in June every year because it's the anniversary of the Stonewall Uprising, an important moment for the Gay Liberation Movement in the United States. On June 28, 1969, the New York City police raided a gay club in Manhattan called the Stonewall Inn, attempting to arrest people for wearing clothing that the police felt was not "appropriate" for their gender. This caused outrage among the community, and they fought back—a riot went on for several days. This unfair treatment by police was publicized and sparked a bigger movement for gay rights in the U.S. and around the world.

## PRISON INDUSTRIAL COMPLEX

### PRIH zun – in DUH stree al – KOHM plex • noun

the idea that businesses and the government rely on the money and services they get from prisons and the system set up to put people in prison

## PRIVILEGE

### PRIHV ledj or PRIH veh ledj • noun

a benefit or opportunity that is given to some people and not others

*A person can be privileged because of forces that are out of their control, like who their parents are or what country they were born in

## PROACTIVE

### proh ACK tiv • adjective

describes taking action to prepare for a situation or getting ready for a future event or problem

## WHAT ARE YOUR PRONOUNS?

Don't assume that you know what someone's pronoun is based on other information you have about them. Even if an individual is part of a group, that doesn't mean that they are exactly like everyone else in that group. So what's the best way to figure out how to address someone? Ask them! In the kindest way possible.

## PROFILING

### PROH fye ling • noun

the assumption that a person is more likely to commit a crime based on what they look like or what they are doing

## PRONOUN

### PRO naun • noun

words like she/her, they/them, or he/him that are used as substitutes for a person's name

## PROTEST

### PROH test • noun

a group of people gathered to object to or to express their disapproval of something

## PUBLIC POLICY

### PUH blik – PAH luh see • noun

rules from or plans made by the government that affect everyone

## QUEER

**KWEER • adjective**

gay, or relating to sexual or romantic love that is not limited to orientation or identity

*Queer is now used as a neutral or positive term, especially when it is used by someone to describe themselves. However, it also has history as a slur (see page 49), so it should be used with caution and only when someone has stated their desire to be identified as queer.*

## QUESTIONING

**KWESS chuh ning • adjective**

describes someone who is not sure what their sexual identity or orientation is

## RACE

**RAYCE • noun**

any group of human beings with common physical traits, such as skin color, or who come from the same culture, religion, location, or language

## RACISM

**RAY sih sem • noun**

discrimination against someone because of their race, or the belief that one race is better than another race

## RECIPROCATE

**re SIH pro kayt • verb**

to give someone something (or to do something for them) in return for something they gave you

## RECKONING

REH kun ing • noun

a time of judgment when past actions are determined to be bad or good and punishments or rewards are given

## RECLAIM

ree CLAYM • verb

to take something back, to take possession of, or to return to an original state

## REDLINING

RED lye ning • noun

an illegal practice of refusing to give loans or money, or practicing unfair money lending, to individuals because of their race or ethnicity

*This practice is called redlining because money lenders would literally draw a red line on a map to mark the neighborhoods they didn't want to invest in. Usually it was Black, inner-city communities that were discriminated against.*

## REFORM

ree FORM • verb

to change something for the better

## REFUGEE

REH fyoo gee • noun

someone who is seeking safe harbor in another place because of an oppressive situation in their home country; someone who runs from their home country for safety

## RENEWABLE ENERGY

ree NOO ah bul – EN er gee • noun

energy to power our world, taken from natural processes that cannot run out of resources

*Examples of renewable energy are sunlight, wind, and geothermal heat (heat from inside the earth).*

## REPARATIONS

reh pah RAY shuns • noun

the act of making things right or giving resources or payment to someone who was injured or wronged in the past

## REPRESENTATION

reh preh zen TAY shun • noun

the state of having all different types of people (races, ethnicities, abilities, religions, identities, and so on) accounted for and included (see Representation Matters!, page 46)

*It's important to see all different types of people represented in culture and media. Seeing a role model who looks just like you can be powerful; seeing a role model who looks different than you can help you understand and empathize with them.*

## REPRESENTATIVE

reh prih ZEN tah tiv • noun

someone who stands in for a group, or someone who is made a leader to represent a group

## RESERVATION

reh sur VAY shun • noun

an area of land that is kept separate for Indigenous North Americans to live on

## RESILIENCE

reh ZIL yen(t)s • noun

the quality of being adaptable to change or hardship

## RESIST

rih ZIST • verb

to oppose, forcefully fight against, or avoid doing something

## RESISTANCE

rih ZIST un(t)z • noun

a group of people organized to challenge something

## RESOURCES

REE sor sez • noun

something available for support or aid, such as money or food

## RESPECT

reh SPEKT • noun

the act of holding someone or something in high regard and giving attention to that person or thing

## RESPONSIBILITY

rih spahn(t) suh BIH lih tee • noun

the state of being called on to answer for your own conduct; accountability

# Representation Matters!

When **Marley Dias** was in fifth grade, she noticed that none of the books she was reading in her classroom centered around characters of color. Many of the main characters were white boys.

She knew that books featuring diverse protagonists, especially young Black girls, were crucial. Not only would young Black girls be able to see themselves as the heroes in a story, but non-Black kids would be able to see beyond stereotypes as well.

"When there are characters that look like you," Marley said, "you can feel as though you also could do these same amazing things."

So she started #1000BlackGirlBooks, a hashtag campaign calling for representation in children's literature. She has collected a database of tens of thousands of books featuring young Black girls as the main character. And to top it all off, she's added a book of her own to the mix: *Marley Dias Gets It Done: And So Can You!*

## RESTORATIVE JUSTICE

**reh STOR ah tiv – JUSS tiss • noun**

the act of repairing harm done and making amends by including everyone in the community, especially helping someone own the crime they committed and making it right for the victims of the crime

## RETRIBUTION

**reh trih BYOO shun • noun**

punishments given out in revenge

## RHETORIC

**REH toh rik • noun**

skillful speaking and writing; can be a negative if the language used is dishonest or meant to manipulate

## RIGHTS

**RYTES • noun**

basic freedoms or things someone is allowed to do, have, or be, just because they are alive

## RIOT

**RYE uht • noun**

violent and uncontrolled actions or disturbances by a group in public

## ROLE

**ROHL • noun**

a job or part someone plays in a group

## ROLE MODEL

**ROHL – MAH dul • noun**

a person to look up to who is a good example

## ROOTS

**ROOTS • noun**

where you came from, your ancestry or history

# S

## SAFE SPACE
**SAYF – SPAYSE • noun**

a physical or metaphorical place where it is accepted and not dangerous to be or to express yourself

## SAFETY
**SAYF tee • noun**

the condition of being free from harm or danger

## SANITATION
**sah nih TAY shun • noun**

the process of discarding human waste in a way that keeps people healthy and safe

*Dignified sanitation services are not available everywhere. Just like access to clean water is an essential human right, access to safe sanitation services can reduce disease and even improve the number of people going to school and going to work in the community.*

## SCHOOL-TO-PRISON PIPELINE
**SKOOL – TO – PRIH zun – PYPE lyne • noun**

the process by which students are criminalized and removed from school to enter the prison system instead of being offered counseling and education

## SEGREGATION
**seh grih GAY shun • noun**

the act of separating people who are different races, classes, or ethnicities, especially to discriminate against one or more of those groups

## SELF-AWARENESS

self – ah WEAR nes • noun

being aware of your own personality, strengths, weaknesses, actions, state of mind, and emotions (and so on) and how your traits or actions might have an effect on others

## SELF-CARE

self – KEYR • noun

taking time to make sure your own physical and mental health needs are taken care of

## SELF-ESTEEM

self – eh STEEM • noun

confidence, respect for, and belief in yourself

## SELF-REFLECTION

self – ree FLEK shun • noun

the ability to look back on your own words, thoughts, beliefs, or actions and examine them

## SENSITIVE

SEN(T) sih tive • adjective

easily or strongly affected, aware of, and able to understand the needs and emotions of others

## SENSITIVITY

sen(t) sih TIV ih tee • noun

the quality of being aware of the needs and emotions of others

## SERVICE

SUR viss • noun

acts done for the good of others that do not need to be repaid

## SEX

SEKS • noun

the anatomy (often male or female) someone was born with

## SEXUALITY

sek shoo(w) AL ih tee • noun

the expression of one's sexual identity

## SIT-IN

SIHT – IHN • noun

a form of protest in which people sit in seats or on the floor and refuse to move, especially to protest a segregated place during racial segregation

## SIZEISM

SY zi sem • noun

discrimination of one or more people because of their body size and weight

## SLAVERY

SLAY veh ree • noun

the practice of "owning" people as property and forcing them to work for free

## SLUR

SLER • noun

a word or phrase meant to harm, insult, or shame someone

## SOCIAL JUSTICE

SOH shul – JUSS tiss • noun

the idea that all human beings deserve equal respect, rights, and freedoms

## SOCIETY

suh SY eh tee • noun

a group of people in the same community or who participate in the same activities, practices, or traditions; a group of companions or people in relationships

## SOCIOECONOMIC

**soh see oh ek oh NAH mik • adjective**

having to do with what social group a person is in and what kind of resources they have

## SOLIDARITY

**sah leh DEHR ih tee • noun**

unity with or between groups that have shared goals or desires

## SOVEREIGN

**SAH v(e)ren • adjective**

the quality of having unlimited power or authority over a country

## SPECTRUM

**SPEK trum • noun**

a broad range within a group

## STATUS QUO

**STAH tus – KWO • noun (Latin)**

the current state of things

## STEREOTYPE

**STEH ree oh type • noun**

a fixed set of ideas that represent an exaggerated view of a person or group, indicating that all members of one group are the same

## From Girl Scout to Activist

Growing up in California, Dolores Fernandez (now **Dolores Huerta**) lived in a diverse agricultural community.

Her activism began when she was in high school, influenced by both the Girl Scouts, where she learned that it's important to take care of other people who need help, and by her mother, who saved up her money to buy a 70-room hotel where she frequently welcomed low-wage workers, sometimes letting them stay for free. Her mother also influenced her to think about civil rights—teaching her values of service and faith, and to make life better for other people without expecting a reward.

After high school, Dolores studied education and became a teacher. Many of her students were children of migrant farm workers, laborers who travel around to work on farms. When she saw kids coming to school hungry and without shoes, she was heartbroken.

She thought she could do more to help them outside the classroom, so she founded the Agricultural Workers Association, which organized for farm workers, helped to register voters, and worked with the government to get help for their local communities.

There she met Cesar Chavez, another activist, and together they created the union that became the United Farm Workers of America. They led the strike of grape workers who organized for better wages and conditions from 1965 to 1970, one of the most important strikes in U.S. history.

# STIGMA

STIHG muh • noun

shame, disgrace, or dishonor given by society

# STRIKE

STRYK • noun

a form of protest in which workers stop working in order to make their voices heard (see From Girl Scout to Activist, opposite)

# SUBJECTIVE

suhb JEK tiv • adjective

relating to opinion instead of fact; able to be interpreted differently by different people

# SUFFRAGE

SUH fridj • noun

the right to vote; often refers to the Women's Rights Movement (see Gender Justice, right)

# SUFFRAGETTE

suh frih JET • noun

a woman who fights for women's voting rights

# SYSTEMIC

siss TEHM ic • adjective

having to do with related parts, groups, or individuals who regularly depend on each other or who form a whole

# SYSTEMIC RACISM

siss TEHM ic – RAY sih sem • noun

when policies and practices that exist throughout a society, organization, or government are racist and unjust by default; also called *institutional racism* or *systemic injustice*

# GENDER JUSTICE

Although the Women's Rights Movement refers to the fight for the right to vote—also known as suffrage—in the United States, there are many more rights still at stake for women worldwide.

On a basic level, fighting for women's rights means fighting for all women, regardless of color, country, or creed, to have:

The right to education. Poverty and child marriage can keep girls out of school, as well as laws and other cultural practices that prioritize men's education.

The right to vote. Some places prevent women from getting to the voting site or make it hard to participate in voting.

The right to be healthy and to make decisions about your own body. A woman or nonbinary person has a right to healthcare and to decide whether they want to have children.

The right to equal pay and treatment. Laws that prevent women from owning land or property can also prevent them from living freely and safely.

The right to be safe. Worldwide, at least 30 percent of women and nonbinary individuals experience gender-based violence.

## TABOO

*tah BOO • adjective*

describes something that isn't supposed to be talked about or isn't done according to social norms

## TARGET

*TAHR geht • verb*

to be focused on or to make something or someone the focus of investigation

## TERRORIST

*TARE or ist • noun*

someone who threatens violence and creates fear in order to gain something or make a government do something

## TOKENISM

*TOE kin ih sem • noun*

the practice of making someone a symbol of their community or making a symbolic effort to include a person or group

## TOLERANCE

*TAH leh run(t)s • noun*

the treatment of other people or groups with respect and sympathy even if their beliefs and practices are different than yours

## TONE

*TOHN • noun*

the pitch of someone's voice; the way someone speaks

## TOWN HALL MEETING

*TAUN – HAUL – MEE ting • noun*

a gathering of people in a public place to discuss matters of the community or for elected officials to answer questions from the community

## TOXIC

**TAK sik • adjective**

describes something that is poisonous or can cause injury

## TOXIC POSITIVITY

**TAK sik – pah sih TIV ih tee • noun**

the belief that someone should have a positive attitude no matter how bad a situation is; an irrational or excessive focus on the positive that can dismiss pain or hardship and make grief or loss seem unimportant

**Some examples of toxic positivity are:**

*"You'll get over it."*
*"Don't be so negative."*
*"Other people have it worse than you."*
*"Cheer up!"*

## TRADITION

**trah DIH shun • noun**

an occasion, behavior, custom, story, or other practice handed down from one generation to the next

## TRAFFICKING

**TRA fik ing • noun**

as in human trafficking: the illegal business of buying and selling human beings as possessions

## TRANS

**TRANZ • adjective**

short for *transgender*; describes someone whose gender identity (see page 25) is not the same as the sex they were assigned at birth

## TRANSITION

**tran ZIH shun • noun**

a process that a trans person goes through to embrace and/or embody their gender identity (see Sharing Her Story, right)

## Sharing Her Story

From a very young age, **Jazz Jennings** knew that she was a girl living inside a boy's body. Her real-life experience of being transgender made her famous in 2007, when she sat down to talk about her transition with reporter Barbara Walters at the tender age of six.

Since then, she has become a public figure and advocate for other children who were born into a body with anatomy that doesn't match their gender identity (this is also called gender dysphoria). Jazz coauthored a book about her story, called *I Am Jazz*, starred in a reality show on TLC (also called *I am Jazz*), and, along with her family, started the TransKids Purple Rainbow Foundation.

Jazz says, "Equality is what unites our society, and everyone needs to understand that not only do we all deserve to be loved, but we deserve to love ourselves for who we are. I want to live in a world where everyone has the freedom to be their authentic self."

## TRAUMA

**TRAH** mah • *noun*

an injury or wound (physical or mental) that is inflicted on someone and causes long-term harm

## TRIAL

**TRY** al • *noun*

a formal meeting to provide judgment on something

## TRIGGER

**TRIH** gur • *verb*

to cause someone to relive trauma or to cause an intense emotional reaction

*If something you read or a video you saw reminded you of a scary thing in the past and brought negative emotions to the surface, you could say that it was triggering.*

## TROPE

**TROHP** • *noun*

an overused expression or turn of phrase

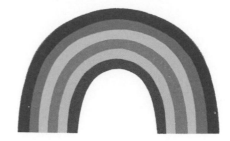

## TWO-SPIRIT

**TOO – SPEER** it • *noun or adjective*

a third gender, or a way to describe a nonbinary individual, in Indigenous North American cultures

## UNCONSCIOUS

uhn KON shus • adjective

not aware of; not awake

## UNCONSCIOUS BIAS

uhn KON shus – BYE us • noun

when you aren't aware that you have a prejudice or judgment toward someone or something

## UNION

YOON yun • noun

referring to a labor union: a group of workers organized to stand up for themselves within their workplace

## UNIQUE

yoo NEEK • adjective

special and unusual; without equal

## UNITY

YOON ih tee • noun

togetherness; oneness; being in harmony with others

## UPHOLD

up HOHLD • verb

to affirm, support, or defend

## VALIDATION

vah lih DAY shun • noun

the act of giving power to something through confirmation; to make something legal or true

## VALUES

VAL yues • noun

a set of moral or ethical beliefs that help you figure out what's right and what's wrong

## VIRTUE

**VER choo • noun**

behavior that is good or moral

*Virtue signaling means talking or posting about your beliefs and values to let others know that you're a good person.*

## VOTE

**VOHT • noun or verb**

*noun:* a wish or choice submitted in a formal way, like with a ballot

*verb:* to cast a ballot to elect someone to office who will work for the people

## VOTER SUPPRESSION

**VOH tur – suh PREH shun • noun**

an effort to keep people from voting by making it hard for them or by taking away their access

*Voter suppression happens a lot more frequently than you might think! Simple laws can make it harder for people to vote, such as getting rid of the option to register to vote on Election Day.*

## VOTING RIGHTS

**VOH ting – RYTES • noun**

the right and ability to participate in elections and have a voice in who gets elected to office; an essential part of democracy

*In the United States, your right to vote also includes your right to vote without being intimidated and your right to have access to polls (where the voting takes place).*

## VULNERABILITY

**vul nur uh BIL ih tee • noun**

the state of being open or emotionally exposed and therefore easily hurt

## WAGE

**WAYJ • noun**

the amount of money someone gets paid for doing a job, often on an hourly basis

## WAGE GAP

**WAYJ – GAAP • noun**

the difference in pay that someone gets for doing the same job as someone else; often used to refer to the gender wage gap, which describes how women get paid less than men to do the same job

## WALKOUT

**WAHK owt • noun**

a strike (see page 51) that happens when workers leave a building or meeting and stop work to show that they disagree

## WATER PROTECTOR

**WAH tur – proh TEK ter • noun**

an activist who is focused on taking care of the earth's water sources (see The Water Warrior, page 58)

## WELFARE

**WEL fair • noun**

public benefits given by the government; also, someone's well-being

## WESTERNIZE

**WEH stur nyz • verb**

to make something conform to or align with values or qualities associated with Western cultures and regions like the United States and Europe

## WHITENESS

WHYTE ness • noun

the quality of being a person with light skin; specifically the way that white people have become advantaged as the dominant culture and the standard or baseline

## WHITE PRIVILEGE

WHYTE – PRIV ledj <u>or</u> PRIH veh ledj • noun

the unearned benefits and advantages that white people get just because they are white

## WHITE SUPREMACY

WHYTE – soo PREM ah see • noun

the idea that the white race is better than other races; also describes the economic, social, and political systems that reinforce this belief of white people as the dominant group

## WHITEWASH

WHYTE wahsh • verb

to change something in a way that favors white people or makes them feel better

*Can also be shortened to wash or washed

## WOMEN'S RIGHTS

WIH minz – RYTES • noun

rights for women that are equal to men's rights (see Gender Justice, page 51)

## WORLDVIEW

WERLD vyew • noun

beliefs that come from seeing or perceiving the world from a particular perspective

## The Water Warrior

Hailing from Wikwemikong Unceded Territory and from Ojibway/Odawa heritage, **Autumn Peltier** is a First Nations Canadian activist.

"Water is everything. It's the lifeblood of Mother Earth. It brings new life," Autumn has said in one of her many talks on climate justice. She has even addressed the United Nations as a keynote speaker. Many Indigenous people live in third world conditions, without safe and clean drinking water, and some communities haven't been able to rely on their water source for decades.

Water protectors like Autumn have also stood up to stop the construction of pipelines that threaten sacred Indigenous land. These pipelines are enormous pathways that allow oil and gas to travel underground from one place to another. While they threaten the water supply, the pipelines can also be devastatingly dangerous if they cause oil spills, gas leaks, or even explosions and fires.

## XENOPHOBIA

**zee no FO bee ah • noun**

fear or hatred of foreigners, immigrants, or anyone thought to be a stranger

## Y'ALL

**YAWL • pronoun**

short for *you all*, a gender-inclusive pronoun used for multiple people

## ZEALOT

**ZELL uht • noun**

someone who has an extreme view or is overly devoted (to a fault) to a cause like religion or politics

## CELEBRATE DIFFERENCES

Learning about and honoring other cultures is one of the best ways to fight xenophobia (and other racist practices). You can:

- Study the art history or creative disciplines of another group of people.

- Watch movies or shows that center other cultures.

- Treat others with kindness.

- Follow someone on social media who looks different than you.

- Support and stand up for all human rights.

# TAKE ACTION!

## "No one is too small to make a difference."
### —Greta Thunberg

Throughout this book, you've read short stories about kids throughout history, and around the world, who took matters into their own hands.

But what causes are YOU passionate about?

Even though you're still in school, you can make a difference in a big or small way.

You can ...

## WRITE A LETTER.

Research how to get in touch with an elected official or a corporation to let them know how you feel about a particular issue. Ask for a specific action.

## MAKE A SIGN.

Pick out a poster or come up with your own slogan or saying to put on a sign. Put it proudly in a window or on your front lawn.

## PARTICIPATE IN A MARCH.

Is there a peaceful protest or rally going on near you for a cause that you support? Look into whether you can attend, ask your parents or guardians whether it's safe to do so, or gather a group that can attend with you. Make sure you bring snacks, water, and the phone number of a responsible adult in case you need help.

## DO SOME MORE RESEARCH.

Look into a cause that really inspires you. Search for books to read, videos to watch, or topics to explore on your own (see the opposite page for a starting point).

Maybe you can take a field trip to a place nearby or visit the website of a museum in a town far away!

## SHARE WHAT YOU KNOW.

Talk to other people, use social media, write an article, make a video or a book! Engage with someone about your newfound knowledge.

# FURTHER READING

## Books

*Generation Brave: The Gen Z Kids Who Are Changing the World*
by Kate Alexander, illustrated by Jade Orlando
Andrews McMeel, 2020

*I Am Jazz*
by Jessica Herthel and Jazz Jennings
Dial Books, 2020

*Kid Activists: True Tales of Childhood from Champions of Change*
stories by Robin Stevenson, illustrated by Allison Steinfeld
Quirk, 2019

*March: Book One, Book Two, and Book Three (a trilogy)*
by John Lewis
Top Shelf Productions, 2013, 2015, and 2016

*Marley Dias Gets It Done: And So Can You!*
by Marley Dias
Scholastic, 2018

*Stamped: Racism, Anti-Racism, and You*
by Jason Reynolds and Dr. Ibram X. Kendi
Little, Brown and Company, 2020

*The Youngest Marcher: The Story of Audrey Faye Hendricks*
by Cynthia Levinson, illustrated by Vanessa Brantley-Newton
Atheneum Books for Young Readers, 2017

*This Is Your Time*
by Ruby Bridges
Delacorte Press, 2020

*Together We March: 25 Protest Movements that Marched into History*
by Leah Henderson, illustrated by Tyler Feder
Atheneum Books for Young Readers, 2021

*You Are Mighty: A Guide to Changing the World*
by Caroline Paul, illustrated by Lauren Tamaki
Bloomsbury Children's Books, 2018

## Museum Websites

National Museum of African American History
https://nmaahc.si.edu

George Washington Carver Museum and Cultural Center
https://www.carveraz.org

New York City's Tenement Museum
https://www.tenement.org

A conversation about slavery at Monticello, Thomas Jefferson's home
https://www.monticello.org/slavery/

Diversity and inclusion initiative at the Seattle Children's Museum
https://thechildrensmuseum.org/letstalkrace/

The Conscious Kid, a resource for equity
https://www.theconsciouskid.org

Portraits of African-Americans in the National Portrait Gallery
https://artsandculture.google.com/exhibit/portraits of african americans national-portrait-gallery/xQJisgUMzpY9Lw?hl=en

## Other Online Resources

Students Demand Action, part of Everytown for Gun Safety
https://studentsdemandaction.org

DoSomething, a nonprofit supporting young activists
DoSomething.org

Learning for Justice, an educational resource for systemic injustice
LearningForJustice.org

Interview with Audrey Faye Hendricks at
PBSLearningMedia.org

*These website addresses were accurate at the time this book went to press. Always make sure to check information online for accuracy and reliability.*

Library of Congress Cataloging-in-Publication Data available upon request.

ISBN: 978-1-950500-94-9

duopress books are available at special discounts when purchased in bulk
for sales promotions as well as for fundraising or educational use.
Special editions can be created to specification.
Contact us at hello@duopressbooks.com for more information.

Manufactured in China
10 9 8 7 6 5 4 3 2 1

Duo Press LLC.
8 Market Place, Suite 300
Baltimore, MD 21202

Design and art direction by Alyssa Nassner
Editing by Liz Saunders
Copyediting by Michele Suchomel-Casey

Distributed by Workman Publishing Company, Inc.
Published simultaneously in Canada by Thomas Allen & Son Limited.

To order: hello@duopressbooks.com

www.duopressbooks.com
www.workman.com